MW00899741

# RIDING THE ALGORITHM

## Proven Strategies to Get Trending Online

Daniel D. Lee

★★★★★

# I. INTRODUCTION

Welcome, dear reader. As the CEO of a leading digital marketing firm, I've seen firsthand the transformative power of the digital age. It's an era defined by rapid change, endless possibilities, and above all, the omnipresent algorithms that shape our online experiences.

This book, "Riding the Algorithm: Proven Strategies to Get Trending Online," is born out of my personal journey navigating the complex and often mystifying world of algorithms. It's a journey filled with triumphs, setbacks, and valuable lessons learned along the way.

Understanding algorithms is no longer a luxury; it's a necessity. In the digital age, algorithms dictate what we see, what we don't, and how we interact with the world around us. They are the invisible puppeteers pulling the strings behind the scenes of our favorite social media platforms, search engines, and e-commerce sites.

In this book, I aim to demystify these complex systems and provide you with the tools and strategies to harness their power. Through personal anecdotes and success stories, I hope to inspire you to leverage algorithms to your advantage, whether you're a business owner seeking to boost your online visibility, a marketer aiming to maximize your campaigns' effectiveness, or a curious individual eager to understand the digital world better.

So, let's embark on this journey together. Let's ride the algorithm.

# A. Brief overview of the book

"Riding the Algorithm: Proven Strategies to Get Trending Online" is a comprehensive guide designed to demystify the world of algorithms and help you harness their power to your advantage. This book is the result of years of experience, research, and practical application in the field of digital marketing and technology.

The book is structured into several key sections, each focusing on a specific aspect of algorithms. We start with the basics, explaining what algorithms are and their role in determining content visibility and trending topics. We then delve into the specifics of various platform algorithms, including Google, Facebook, Instagram, Twitter, YouTube, TikTok, and Amazon.

We explore the role of AI and Machine Learning in shaping algorithms and predict their future impact. We also discuss the influence of user behavior on algorithms and provide strategies to leverage this for better visibility. Ethical considerations, such as bias and discrimination in algorithm design, are also addressed.

The book provides a deep dive into the power of SEO, both general and local, and the role of social media algorithms. We emphasize the importance of quality content and discuss strategies for different platforms, including video content. We also explore the importance of data analysis, personalization, paid advertising, and e-commerce in the context of algorithms.

Finally, we discuss how to stay updated with algorithm updates and penalties, and how to prepare for future changes. The book concludes with a recap of key strategies, words of encouragement for the journey ahead, and a list of resources for further reading.

In essence, "Riding the Algorithm" is your comprehensive guide to understanding and leveraging the power of algorithms in the digital age. Whether you're a seasoned professional or a beginner in the digital world, this book aims to equip you with the knowledge and tools you need to navigate the digital landscape effectively and successfully.

## *B. Importance of understanding algorithms in the digital age*

In the digital age, algorithms are the invisible forces that shape our online experiences. They determine what content we see, what products we're recommended, and even who we interact with on social media. Understanding these algorithms is crucial for anyone looking to make an impact online, whether you're a business owner, a marketer, a content creator, or simply an individual trying to navigate the digital world.

Firstly, algorithms play a critical role in visibility. They decide what content gets seen and by whom. If you're a business, understanding how these algorithms work can help you reach your target audience more effectively. If you're a consumer, it can help you find the content and products that are most relevant to you.

Secondly, algorithms are constantly evolving. Major platforms like Google, Facebook, and Instagram regularly update their algorithms to improve user experience and stay ahead of malicious actors. Staying updated with these changes can help you adapt your strategies and stay ahead of the competition.

Thirdly, understanding algorithms can help you make more informed decisions. Whether it's deciding what keywords to target for SEO, what type of content to create, or how to personalize your marketing efforts, a solid understanding of algorithms can guide your decision-making process and increase your chances of success.

Lastly, there are ethical considerations. Algorithms can unintentionally perpetuate biases and discrimination, and understanding how they work can help us identify and address these issues.

In conclusion, understanding algorithms is not just about improving your online visibility or marketing efforts. It's about being an informed and responsible digital citizen. It's about understanding the rules of the digital world so you can navigate it more effectively and ethically. That's what this book aims to help you achieve.

## C. Personal anecdotes
## and success stories

As the CEO of a leading digital marketing firm, I've had the privilege of witnessing the transformative power of algorithms firsthand. Let me share a few personal anecdotes and success stories that underscore the importance of understanding and leveraging algorithms.

One of our earliest clients was a small, family-owned business struggling to make their mark online. Despite having high-quality products and a strong commitment to customer service, their online visibility was virtually non-existent. We worked with them to understand the algorithms of various platforms, particularly Google's search algorithm. By optimizing their website for SEO, targeting the right keywords, and creating valuable content, we were able to significantly increase their online visibility. Within a year, their website traffic had increased by over 200%, and their sales had seen a similar boost.

Another success story involves a non-profit organization that was trying to raise awareness about a particular social issue. They had a strong social media presence, but their posts were not reaching their intended audience. We helped them understand the algorithms of various social media platforms and tailored their content strategy accordingly. By posting at optimal times, engaging with their audience, and using the right hashtags, they were able to increase their reach and engagement significantly. This led to a substantial increase in donations and volunteers for their cause.

These stories are just a few examples of how understanding and leveraging algorithms can lead to real, tangible results. Whether you're a small business looking to increase your online visibility, a non-profit organization trying to spread awareness, or an individual trying to make sense of the digital world, this book is designed to help you ride the algorithm to success.

# II. UNDERSTANDING ALGORITHMS

## A. What is an Algorithm?

Before we delve into the intricacies of leveraging algorithms, it's crucial to understand what an algorithm is at its core. An algorithm, in the simplest terms, is a set of instructions designed to perform a specific task. It's a step-by-step procedure, much like a recipe, that guides a process from start to finish.

In the context of the digital world, algorithms are the backbone of any computational process. They are the rules and procedures a computer follows to solve a problem or achieve a particular goal. From the search results you see on Google to the posts that appear on your Facebook feed, to the recommendations you get on Amazon, algorithms are at work.

Algorithms are not a new concept. They have been around for centuries, used in mathematics and science. However, with the advent of computers and the internet, their role has become significantly more prominent and influential.

In the online world, algorithms are used to sort, organize, and present vast amounts of information in a way that is most relevant, useful, or appealing to the user. They analyze a multitude of factors, such as your past behavior, preferences, location, and what others with similar behaviors and preferences have found interesting.

Understanding algorithms is the first step towards mastering the digital landscape. As we progress through this book, we'll explore how different platforms utilize algorithms and how you can optimize your online presence by aligning with these algorithms. But for now, remember this: an algorithm is a set of rules that a computer follows to achieve a goal. It's the secret sauce that makes the digital world tick.

## B. The Role of Algorithms in Content Visibility and Trending Topics

Algorithms play a pivotal role in determining what content surfaces on our screens and what remains unseen in the vast digital ocean. They are the gatekeepers of information in the online world, deciding what gets visibility and what doesn't.

Every time you perform a search on Google, scroll through your Instagram feed, or watch a video on YouTube, you're interacting with complex algorithms designed to curate an experience tailored to your preferences and behavior. These algorithms analyze a multitude of factors, such as your search history, engagement patterns, location, and even the device you're using, to deliver content they believe will be most relevant and engaging to you.

This personalized curation of content is not just about enhancing user experience. It's also about driving engagement. The more relevant and engaging the content, the more likely users are to interact with it - be it clicking a link, liking a post, sharing a video, or making a purchase. This engagement, in turn, feeds back into the algorithm, influencing future content delivery.

When it comes to trending topics, algorithms play an equally significant role. Trending topics are typically those that are garnering a high level of engagement in a short period. Algorithms identify these spikes in engagement and amplify them by promoting the trending content to more users. This can create a viral effect, where the content spreads rapidly and widely across the platform.

In essence, algorithms are the driving force behind content visibility and trending topics in the digital realm. They shape our online experiences, influence our perceptions, and in many ways, dictate the ebb and flow of digital trends. Understanding their workings is key to navigating the digital landscape effectively and harnessing their power to your advantage.

# III. PLATFORM-SPECIFIC ALGORITHMS

## A. Understanding Google's Algorithm

Google's search algorithm is arguably one of the most influential algorithms in the digital world. It's the gatekeeper to the vast wealth of information available on the internet, determining what content we see when we type a query into the search bar. Understanding how this algorithm works is crucial for anyone looking to improve their online visibility.

At its core, Google's algorithm is designed to provide users with the most relevant and high-quality results for their search queries. It does this by crawling and indexing billions of web pages and then ranking them based on hundreds of different factors.

One of the most important factors is relevance. Google uses sophisticated natural language processing techniques to understand the content of each web page and how well it matches the user's query. This includes looking at the use of keywords in the content, the context in which they're used, and the overall topic of the page.

Another key factor is quality. Google assesses the quality of a web page based on several indicators, such as the authority of the website, the quality of the content, and the user experience. This includes factors like the website's loading speed, mobile-friendliness, and use of intrusive ads.

Google's algorithm also considers the user's location, language, and browsing history to provide personalized results. For example, a search for "pizza" will likely show results for pizza places near the user's current location.

It's important to note that Google's algorithm is constantly evolving. The company regularly updates its algorithm to improve the quality of its search results and to stay ahead of spammy and manipulative practices. Staying updated with these changes is crucial for maintaining and improving your website's visibility in Google's search results.

In the following sections, we'll also explore the algorithms of other major platforms, including Facebook, Instagram, Twitter, YouTube, TikTok, and Amazon. Each platform has its own unique algorithm, and understanding how each one works can help you tailor your strategies and maximize your success on each platform.

## B. Understanding Facebook's Algorithm

Facebook's algorithm, known as the News Feed algorithm, plays a crucial role in determining what content users see when they log into the platform. With billions of posts, photos, and videos being shared on Facebook every day, the algorithm helps to curate a user's News Feed based on their interests and interactions.

At its core, Facebook's algorithm prioritizes content that sparks meaningful interactions between users. It uses a variety of signals to predict what posts a user will find most engaging. Here's a closer look at how it works:

Inventory: The algorithm starts by taking an inventory of all the posts that you could potentially see when you log into Facebook. This includes posts from your friends, groups you belong to, and pages you follow.

Signals: The algorithm then looks at a wide range of signals to determine how interested you might be in each post. These signals include things like who posted the content, how recently it was posted, and your past interactions with the poster. It also includes more specific details about the post itself, such as the type of content (e.g., photo, video, link), the engagement it's received (e.g., likes, comments, shares), and whether it's been reported as spam or false news.

Predictions: Based on these signals, the algorithm makes predictions about how likely you are to interact with the post in different ways (e.g., liking, commenting, sharing, clicking). The goal is to prioritize posts that you're most likely to engage with and that encourage meaningful interactions.

Score: Each post is assigned a relevancy score based on these predictions. The higher the score, the more likely the post is to appear in your News Feed.

Personalization: The algorithm also personalizes your News Feed based on your preferences. For example, if you often watch videos or interact with photos, you'll likely see more of this type of content. Similarly, if you frequently engage with posts from a particular friend or page, you'll see more of their posts.

It's important to note that Facebook's algorithm is constantly evolving. The company regularly updates its algorithm to improve the user experience and address issues like misinformation and harmful content. Understanding how the algorithm works can help you create content that resonates with your audience and achieves higher visibility on the platform.

# C. Understanding Instagram's Algorithm

Instagram's algorithm, much like Facebook's, is designed to predict what content users will find most engaging and display that content prominently in their feeds. Understanding this algorithm is vital for anyone looking to increase their visibility or engagement on the platform. Here's a closer look at how it works:

Interest: The Instagram algorithm predicts what posts you'll care about most based on your past behavior. If you've liked, commented on, or shared similar content in the past, the algorithm is more likely to show you that type of content in the future.

Recency: The algorithm also considers how recently the post was shared. More recent posts are more likely to appear in your feed than older ones, although this doesn't mean that Instagram shows posts in chronological order.

Relationship: The algorithm prioritizes posts from accounts that you interact with regularly. If you frequently like or comment on someone's posts, or if you're tagged in photos together, the algorithm recognizes that you have a relationship with that person and is more likely to show you their content.

Frequency: The algorithm also takes into account how often you open Instagram. If you're a frequent user, your feed will look more chronological because the algorithm tries to show you the best posts since your last visit.

Following: If you follow a lot of people, Instagram will try to show you a bit of content from all of them. If you follow fewer people, you'll see more of each person's posts.

Usage: The algorithm also considers how long you spend on

Instagram. If you spend a lot of time on the app, you'll dig deeper into your feed and see more content, while if you spend less time, you'll get highlights from the algorithm.

Instagram's algorithm is constantly learning and adapting based on your behavior. The more you use the platform, the better it understands your preferences and the better it can tailor your feed to your interests.

In the following sections of the book, we'll provide more detailed strategies for optimizing your content for Instagram's algorithm, as well as the algorithms of other major platforms. Each platform has its own unique algorithm, and understanding how each one works can help you tailor your strategies and maximize your success on each platform.

## D. Understanding Twitter's Algorithm

Twitter's algorithm plays a significant role in determining what tweets users see in their timeline. Unlike the chronological feed of the past, Twitter's current algorithm is designed to show users the most relevant tweets first, based on a variety of factors. Here's a closer look at how it works:

Recency: Similar to other platforms, Twitter's algorithm considers the recency of a tweet. Newer tweets are more likely to appear at the top of your timeline.

Engagement: The algorithm also considers the level of engagement a tweet has received, including likes, retweets, replies, and clicks. Tweets that have received more engagement are more likely to appear at the top of your timeline.

Relevance: The algorithm predicts what tweets are most relevant to you based on your past activity. This includes the tweets you've interacted with, the topics you're interested in, and the accounts you follow.

Behavior: The algorithm takes into account your behavior on Twitter, including who you follow, who you interact with, and what tweets you engage with. It uses this information to predict what content you'll find most interesting.

Network: The algorithm also considers the activity of people you're connected to. If people you follow engage with a tweet, the algorithm is more likely to show you that tweet.

Twitter's algorithm is constantly evolving, with regular updates to improve the user experience and provide more relevant content. Understanding how the algorithm works can help you create content that resonates with your audience and achieves higher visibility on the platform.

# E. Understanding YouTube's Algorithm

YouTube's algorithm plays a critical role in determining what videos appear in a user's feed, recommended videos, and search results. It's designed to provide users with the most relevant and engaging content based on their viewing habits and preferences. Here's a closer look at how it works:

Performance Metrics: The algorithm considers various performance metrics of a video, including view count, watch time, likes, dislikes, shares, comments, and the percentage of a video that's watched (also known as audience retention).

Relevance: The algorithm also considers the relevance of a video to a user's search query or viewing history. This includes the title, description, tags, and even the transcript of the video.

User Behavior: The algorithm takes into account a user's past behavior, including their search history, viewing history, and interactions (such as likes, dislikes, and comments). It uses this information to predict what videos a user will find most interesting.

Engagement: The algorithm prioritizes videos that drive engagement. This includes not only likes, comments, and shares, but also whether a video drives users to subscribe, click on another video, or visit an external website.

Session Time: The algorithm also considers how a video contributes to a user's overall session time on YouTube. Videos that keep users on the platform for longer are more likely to be recommended.

YouTube's algorithm is constantly learning and adapting based on user behavior. The more a user interacts with the platform, the better the algorithm becomes at understanding their preferences and recommending relevant content.

## F. Understanding TikTok's Algorithm

TikTok's algorithm, often referred to as the "For You" algorithm, is a powerful tool that determines what content appears on a user's "For You" page - the main feed of the app. This algorithm is designed to deliver personalized content that aligns with a user's interests and engagement patterns. Here's a closer look at how it works:

User Interactions: The algorithm takes into account the videos you've liked or shared, the accounts you follow, the content you create, and the comments you post. It uses this information to understand your preferences and show you more of what you enjoy.

Video Information: This includes details about the videos you watch, such as the details of the video itself (like hashtags, details in the description, and the genre of the video) and the popularity of the video. If you often engage with a certain type of content or a trending topic, the algorithm is more likely to show you similar content.

Device and Account Settings: Information about your device and account settings also plays a role in personalization. This includes details like your location, language preference, and device type. However, TikTok has stated that these factors carry less weight than the others because they don't reflect personal preference types.

TikTok's algorithm uses a recommendation system that adapts to each user's unique preferences over time. The more you use the app and interact with content, the better the algorithm gets at understanding your preferences and delivering content that you'll enjoy.

## G. Understanding Amazon's Shopping Recommendation System

Amazon's shopping recommendation system is a powerful algorithm that plays a significant role in the online shopping experience. It's designed to suggest products that a user might be interested in based on their browsing history, purchase history, items in their shopping cart, and items that other customers have bought. Here's a closer look at how it works:

Browsing History: The algorithm takes into account the products you've viewed while browsing Amazon. It uses this information to recommend similar products that you might be interested in.

Purchase History: The algorithm also considers your past purchases. It uses this information to recommend other products that are often bought together with the items you've purchased.

Shopping Cart: The items in your shopping cart also influence the recommendations. The algorithm suggests related products that you might want to add to your cart.

Customer Behavior: Amazon's algorithm also takes into account the behavior of other customers. It looks at what other customers have viewed and purchased, especially those who have shown similar preferences to you.

Ratings and Reviews: The algorithm also considers the ratings and reviews of products. Products with higher ratings and positive reviews are more likely to be recommended.

Amazon's shopping recommendation system is a powerful tool for personalizing the shopping experience. It helps customers discover new products they might like, and it helps sellers increase their visibility and sales.

# IV. THE ROLE OF AI AND MACHINE LEARNING IN ALGORITHMS

# A. Understanding AI and Machine Learning

Artificial Intelligence (AI) and Machine Learning (ML) are two terms that have become increasingly prevalent in our digital vocabulary. They represent a significant shift in the way we approach problem-solving and decision-making in the digital realm, and they play a crucial role in the functioning and evolution of algorithms.

Artificial Intelligence, at its core, is the concept of machines being able to carry out tasks in a way that we would consider "smart." It's about creating systems that can perform tasks that would normally require human intelligence, such as understanding natural language, recognizing patterns, solving problems, and making decisions.

Machine Learning, a subset of AI, takes this concept a step further. It's a method of data analysis that automates the building of analytical models. In other words, it's a way of "teaching" machines to learn from data and improve their performance over time without being explicitly programmed to do so.

The idea is to feed the machine a large amount of data and let it learn the underlying patterns and relationships within that data. The machine can then use this learned knowledge to make predictions or decisions without being explicitly programmed to perform the task.

For example, a machine learning model could be trained on a dataset of customer behavior and purchase history. The model would learn the patterns and relationships in the data, such as which products are often bought together or what kind of customers are more likely to make a purchase. This learned knowledge can then be used to make predictions, such as recommending products to customers based on their behavior.

In the context of algorithms, AI and ML are game-changers. They enable algorithms to learn from data, adapt to changes, and make more accurate and personalized decisions. This leads to more relevant and engaging content delivery, better user experience, and ultimately, higher engagement and conversion rates. As we delve deeper into the role of AI and ML in algorithms, we'll explore how they shape the digital landscape and how you can leverage their power to your advantage.

## B. How AI and Machine Learning
## Shape Algorithms

Artificial Intelligence and Machine Learning have revolutionized the way algorithms function, making them more dynamic, adaptable, and efficient. They've transformed algorithms from static sets of instructions into learning entities that can improve and refine their operations over time.

Here's how AI and Machine Learning shape algorithms:

Adaptability: Traditional algorithms follow a fixed set of instructions, which means they perform the same way unless manually updated or changed. However, algorithms powered by Machine Learning can adapt based on the data they process. They learn from the patterns and trends in the data, allowing them to adjust their behavior and improve their performance over time. This adaptability is crucial in the ever-evolving digital landscape where user behavior, market trends, and content strategies are constantly changing.

Personalization: AI and Machine Learning enable algorithms to deliver highly personalized content. By analyzing a user's behavior, preferences, and interaction history, these algorithms can predict what content a user is likely to find interesting or relevant. This level of personalization enhances user experience and engagement, leading to higher click-through rates, longer session durations, and increased conversions.

Predictive Analysis: Machine Learning algorithms can identify patterns and trends in large datasets and use this information to make predictions about future behavior. This predictive capability is widely used in areas like user behavior analysis, trend forecasting, and demand prediction. It allows businesses to anticipate user needs, stay ahead of market trends, and make data-driven decisions.

Efficiency and Accuracy: AI and Machine Learning can process and analyze vast amounts of data much faster and more accurately than humanly possible. This efficiency and accuracy are vital in the digital world, where billions of data points are generated every second. It allows algorithms to deliver timely and accurate content, enhancing user experience and driving engagement.

Continuous Learning: Perhaps the most significant advantage of AI and Machine Learning is their ability to learn continuously. As they process more data, they learn more, improving their performance and accuracy over time. This continuous learning capability allows algorithms to stay updated and relevant, even in the face of changing user behavior and market trends.

In conclusion, AI and Machine Learning have fundamentally reshaped algorithms, making them more adaptable, personalized, predictive, efficient, and continuously learning. They've turned algorithms from mere tools into strategic assets that can drive engagement, growth, and success in the digital world. As we move forward, understanding and leveraging the power of AI and Machine Learning in algorithms will be key to staying competitive and achieving success online.

## C. Future Predictions: AI's Impact on Algorithms

As we look towards the future, it's clear that the impact of Artificial Intelligence on algorithms will continue to grow. The fusion of AI and algorithms is set to redefine the digital landscape, driving innovation and transformation in unprecedented ways. Here are some predictions on how AI might shape algorithms in the future:

Increased Personalization: As AI becomes more sophisticated, we can expect even greater levels of personalization. Algorithms will be able to understand user preferences and behaviors with remarkable accuracy, delivering highly personalized content, recommendations, and experiences. This could extend beyond digital platforms to areas like personalized education, healthcare, and retail experiences.

Real-time Adaptability: Future algorithms will be able to adapt in real-time, responding instantly to changes in user behavior, market trends, and other factors. This will allow for more timely and relevant content delivery, enhancing user experience and engagement.

Predictive and Prescriptive Analytics: AI-powered algorithms will not only predict future behavior based on past data but will also be able to prescribe optimal actions to achieve specific goals. This could revolutionize areas like digital marketing, where algorithms could suggest the best strategies to increase engagement or conversions.

Ethical and Fair Algorithms: As awareness about the ethical implications of AI grows, there will be increased focus on creating fair and transparent algorithms. This could lead to the development of AI models that can detect and mitigate bias, ensuring that algorithms treat all users fairly and equitably.

Autonomous Decision-Making: As AI and Machine Learning technologies advance, algorithms may gain the ability to make complex decisions autonomously. This could have significant implications in areas like autonomous vehicles, financial trading, and healthcare, where algorithms could make real-time decisions based on a multitude of factors.

Improved Human-AI Interaction: Future algorithms will be better at understanding and interacting with humans. This could lead to more natural and intuitive human-AI interactions, with algorithms understanding not just explicit commands, but also implicit cues like tone, context, and emotion.

In conclusion, the future of algorithms is intertwined with the evolution of AI. As AI continues to advance, it will bring about profound changes in the way algorithms function and the role they play in our lives. Embracing this future will require not just technical understanding, but also a thoughtful consideration of the ethical, societal, and human implications of these technologies.

# V. USER BEHAVIOR AND ALGORITHMS

## A. The Impact of User Behavior on Algorithms

User behavior plays a critical role in shaping algorithms. In fact, it's one of the primary factors that algorithms use to make decisions. Every click, like, share, comment, search query, and even the amount of time you spend on a page or video, is a piece of data that algorithms analyze to understand your preferences and behaviors.

Here's how user behavior impacts algorithms:

Personalization: Algorithms use user behavior data to personalize the content they deliver. If you frequently watch cooking videos on YouTube, the algorithm will learn from this behavior and show you more cooking-related content. Similarly, if you often search for tech news on Google, the algorithm will prioritize tech news in your future search results.

Relevance Ranking: User behavior data helps algorithms determine the relevance of content. For instance, if a particular article is being clicked on frequently in search results, the algorithm will consider it more relevant and rank it higher.

Recommendation Systems: User behavior is key to recommendation systems on platforms like Amazon and Netflix.

These algorithms analyze your past behavior (e.g., products you've bought, movies you've watched) to recommend similar items you might like.

Trending Topics: Algorithms use user behavior to identify trending topics. If a particular hashtag is being used frequently on Twitter, or a video is getting a lot of views on TikTok, the algorithm will recognize this behavior and may promote the topic or video more widely.

Ad Targeting: Ad algorithms use user behavior to target ads effectively. If you've been searching for running shoes, you might start seeing ads for running shoes on various platforms.

Feedback Loop: User behavior creates a feedback loop that continuously influences and is influenced by algorithms. When an algorithm shows you certain content based on your past behavior, your interaction with that content feeds back into the algorithm, influencing what it shows you in the future.

In essence, user behavior is the fuel that powers algorithms. It's the raw data that algorithms use to learn, adapt, and deliver personalized, relevant content. Understanding this relationship between user behavior and algorithms is key to leveraging algorithms effectively.

## B. Strategies to Leverage User Behavior for Better Visibility

Understanding the impact of user behavior on algorithms is one thing, but leveraging this knowledge to gain better visibility online is another. Here are some strategies that can help you align with user behavior and optimize your content for algorithms:

Create Engaging Content: The more engaging your content, the more likely users are to interact with it - be it through likes, shares, comments, or time spent on page. These interactions signal to the algorithm that your content is valuable, leading to better visibility.

Understand Your Audience: Use analytics tools to understand your audience's behavior - what they like, what they share, when they are most active, etc. Tailor your content and posting schedule to align with these behaviors.

Optimize for Search Intent: When it comes to search algorithms, understanding user intent is key. Try to understand what users are looking for when they use certain search terms and create content that meets those needs.

Encourage User Engagement: Encourage users to interact with your content. This could be through compelling calls to action, engaging questions, interactive elements, or incentives for sharing your content.

Use Relevant Keywords: Keywords are a crucial factor in how algorithms understand content. Use relevant keywords in your content, but make sure to do so naturally and in a way that aligns with your audience's search intent.

Leverage Social Proof: Algorithms consider social proof, like reviews and testimonials, as indicators of quality. Encourage users to leave reviews or share their experiences with your brand.

Stay Current with Algorithm Updates: Algorithms are constantly evolving. Stay updated with these changes and adapt your strategies accordingly.

Remember, the goal is not to 'game' the algorithm, but to understand how user behavior influences it and use this understanding to create a better user experience. When you focus on the user, better visibility will follow.

# C. Case Studies: Successful
## User Behavior Analysis

Understanding the theory behind user behavior and algorithms is important, but seeing these principles in action can provide valuable insights. Let's look at a few case studies where successful user behavior analysis led to significant improvements in visibility and engagement.

Netflix's Personalized Recommendations: Netflix is a prime example of a company that has mastered the art of user behavior analysis. By analyzing user behavior data (such as viewing history, ratings, and browsing habits), Netflix's algorithms can recommend shows and movies that users are likely to enjoy. This personalized approach has led to high user engagement and retention rates.

Amazon's 'Customers Who Bought This Item Also Bought' Feature: Amazon's recommendation algorithm uses user behavior data to suggest products that customers might be interested in based on their past purchases and browsing history. This feature not only enhances the user experience but also drives additional sales.

Spotify's Discover Weekly Playlist: Spotify's Discover Weekly playlist is a personalized playlist that's updated every week with songs that the algorithm predicts the user will enjoy. The algorithm analyzes the user's listening history, favorite genres, and playlists, as well as the listening habits of other users with similar tastes. This feature has been a huge hit, with millions of users tuning in every week.

Google's RankBrain Algorithm: Google's RankBrain is a machine learning-based algorithm that helps Google understand search queries and deliver more relevant search results. By analyzing user behavior data (like click-through rates and dwell time), RankBrain can learn which results are most relevant for a given query and adjust the rankings accordingly.

These case studies demonstrate the power of user behavior analysis in shaping algorithms and driving engagement. By understanding and responding to user behavior, these companies have been able to deliver personalized, relevant experiences that keep users coming back for more.

# VI. THE ETHICS OF ALGORITHMS

## A. The Dark Side of Algorithms:
## Bias and Discrimination

While algorithms have revolutionized the way we interact with digital platforms, they are not without their flaws. One of the most significant ethical concerns surrounding algorithms is the potential for bias and discrimination.

Algorithms are designed and programmed by humans, and they learn from data that is generated by humans. As a result, they can inadvertently perpetuate and amplify human biases. If the data used to train an algorithm contains biases, the algorithm is likely to learn and replicate those biases.

For example, if a job recruitment algorithm is trained on data from a company where men have historically been preferred for certain roles, the algorithm might learn to favor male candidates. Similarly, if a facial recognition algorithm is primarily trained on images of light-skinned individuals, it might perform poorly when identifying individuals with darker skin tones.

Bias in algorithms can lead to discrimination and unfair treatment. It can affect a wide range of areas, from job recruitment and credit scoring to law enforcement and healthcare. It can disadvantage certain groups of people based on their race, gender, age, or other characteristics.

Addressing bias in algorithms is a complex and ongoing challenge. It requires a combination of diverse data sets, transparent algorithm design, rigorous testing, and continuous monitoring and adjustment. It also requires a commitment to ethical principles and fairness.

In the following sections of the book, we'll delve deeper into the issue of bias in algorithms and explore strategies for mitigating it. We'll also discuss other ethical considerations in algorithm design, such as privacy and accountability. Understanding the ethical implications of algorithms is crucial for anyone looking to use them responsibly and effectively.

# B. Ethical Considerations
## in Algorithm Design

When designing and implementing algorithms, it's crucial to consider the ethical implications. Algorithms have the power to shape our digital experiences, influence our decisions, and impact our lives in significant ways. Here are some key ethical considerations in algorithm design:

Fairness: Algorithms should be designed to treat all users fairly and not discriminate based on characteristics like race, gender, age, or socioeconomic status. This requires using diverse and representative data sets for training algorithms and regularly testing algorithms for bias.

Transparency: There should be transparency about how algorithms work and how they make decisions. While the technical details of algorithms might be complex, users should be able to understand the basic principles behind an algorithm's decisions.

Accountability: There should be mechanisms in place to hold algorithms (and the people and organizations behind them) accountable for their decisions. If an algorithm causes harm or makes a mistake, there should be a way to address the issue and prevent it from happening again.

Privacy: Algorithms often rely on personal data to make decisions. It's crucial to respect user privacy and use personal data responsibly. This includes obtaining informed consent from users, anonymizing data, and implementing robust data security measures.

Beneficence: Algorithms should be designed to benefit users and society as a whole. They should improve the user experience, provide valuable services, and contribute to societal good.

Ethical algorithm design is not just about avoiding harm —it's about actively promoting good. It's about ensuring that algorithms respect human rights, promote fairness, and contribute to a better digital world. In the following sections of the book, we'll explore these ethical considerations in more detail and provide strategies for ethical algorithm design and use.

# C. Advocacy and Change:
## Promoting Fair Algorithms

Promoting fair algorithms is not just the responsibility of those who design and implement them—it's a collective effort that requires advocacy and change at multiple levels. Here's how we can all contribute to promoting fair algorithms:

Raise Awareness: One of the first steps towards promoting fair algorithms is raising awareness about the issue. This includes educating people about how algorithms work, the potential for bias and discrimination, and the impact of algorithms on our lives.

Demand Transparency: As users of digital platforms, we can demand greater transparency about how algorithms make decisions. This includes asking platforms to disclose the principles and practices behind their algorithms and to provide users with more control over how algorithms affect their experiences.

Support Regulation: We can also support regulations that promote fairness, transparency, and accountability in algorithms. This includes laws and regulations that require algorithmic audits, protect user privacy, and prevent discriminatory practices.

Promote Diversity in Tech: Promoting diversity in the tech industry can also help mitigate algorithmic bias. A diverse workforce brings a wider range of perspectives and experiences, which can lead to more inclusive and fair algorithms.

Use Ethical Tech: As consumers, we can choose to use and support tech companies that prioritize ethical algorithm design. By voting with our wallets, we can encourage more companies to commit to fairness, transparency, and accountability in their algorithms.

Promoting fair algorithms is a complex and ongoing challenge, but it's a challenge worth taking on. By advocating for change and supporting ethical tech, we can help ensure that algorithms serve us all fairly and effectively. In the following sections of the book, we'll delve deeper into these strategies and explore how we can all contribute to promoting fair algorithms.

# VII. THE POWER
# OF SEO

# A. Introduction to SEO

Search Engine Optimization, or SEO, is one of the most powerful tools in the digital marketer's arsenal. It's the practice of optimizing your online content so that a search engine likes to show it as a top result for searches of a certain keyword.

In the vast digital landscape, visibility is key. And when it comes to visibility on the internet, search engines rule the roost. Google alone processes over 3.5 billion searches per day. That's a lot of people looking for answers, products, services, or information. SEO is about ensuring that when people search for something that aligns with your content, it's your website that shows up in the search results, not your competitor's.

SEO involves a variety of strategies and techniques, all aimed at improving your site's visibility in search engine results. These include keyword research and optimization, creating high-quality and engaging content, improving site speed and mobile-friendliness, building high-quality backlinks, and more.

But SEO is not just about driving traffic to your site. It's about attracting the right kind of traffic. It's about understanding what your target audience is searching for, how they're searching for it, and making sure that it's your content that meets their needs.

In the following sections, we'll delve deeper into the world of SEO, exploring various strategies and techniques, and how you can leverage them to improve your online visibility. Whether you're a seasoned digital marketer or a business owner looking to grow your online presence, understanding the power of SEO is a crucial step in your journey.

# B. Keyword Research and Optimization

Keyword research and optimization is a fundamental aspect of SEO. It's about identifying the words and phrases that people use when they search for information online, and then optimizing your content around these keywords to improve its visibility in search engine results.

Here's a step-by-step guide on how to conduct keyword research and optimization:

Identify Your Niche: Before you start your keyword research, it's important to have a clear understanding of your niche, your target audience, and what kind of content they might be searching for.

Brainstorm Initial Keywords: Think about the main categories of your business and list down all the relevant topics. Then, brainstorm potential keywords for each topic. These are the words or phrases that you think your target audience might use when searching for your products, services, or content.

Use Keyword Research Tools: Tools like Google Keyword Planner, SEMrush, and Ahrefs can help you find more keyword ideas, see how often certain keywords are searched, and how competitive these keywords are. This can help you identify high-volume, low-competition keywords that you have a good chance of ranking for.

Analyze Your Competitors: Look at the keywords your competitors are targeting. This can give you ideas for keywords that you might have missed, and help you understand what kind of keywords are effective in your industry.

Choose Your Keywords: Based on your research, choose the keywords that are most relevant to your content, have a good search volume, and are not too competitive.

Optimize Your Content: Once you've chosen your keywords, it's time to optimize your content. Include your keywords in important places like the title, meta description, headings, and body of the content. But remember, your primary goal is to provide valuable content to your readers, so make sure your use of keywords feels natural and doesn't compromise the quality of your content.

Monitor and Adjust: SEO is not a one-time thing. It's important to monitor your results, see how your content is ranking for your chosen keywords, and adjust your strategy as needed.

Remember, the goal of keyword research and optimization is not just to increase traffic to your site, but to attract the right kind of traffic. By understanding and targeting the keywords your audience is using, you can ensure that your content is found by the people who will find it most valuable.

# C. On-Page and Off-Page SEO

SEO can be broadly divided into two categories: On-Page SEO and Off-Page SEO. Both are crucial to improving your website's visibility in search engine results, but they involve different strategies and techniques.

On-Page SEO refers to the actions you take on your own website to improve its search engine rankings. This includes:

Keyword Optimization: As discussed earlier, this involves researching and using relevant keywords in your content.

Content Quality: Creating high-quality, engaging, and valuable content is crucial. This not only helps to keep visitors on your site longer but also increases the chances of them sharing your content, both of which can improve your rankings.

Meta Tags: These are snippets of text that describe a page's content and appear in the page's code. They don't appear on the page itself but in the search engine results. This includes the meta title and meta description, both of which should include your target keywords.

URL Structure: URLs should be simple, readable, and keyword-rich. A good URL structure not only provides both users and search engines with more information about the page but also improves the chances of a higher ranking.

Internal Linking: Linking to other pages on your website helps search engines understand the content of your site, and can also keep visitors on your site longer.

Off-Page SEO, on the other hand, refers to actions taken outside of your own website to impact your rankings within search engine results pages. This includes:

Backlinks: These are links from other websites to your site. They are one of the most important factors in how search engines rank sites. The more high-quality backlinks you have, the more credible your site appears to search engines.

Social Signals: While not a direct ranking factor, there's a correlation between social signals (like shares, likes, and comments on social media) and ranking position. A strong social presence can boost your SEO.

Guest Blogging: Writing posts for other websites can help you reach a wider audience and gain more backlinks.

Influencer Outreach: Collaborating with influencers in your industry can help you reach a wider audience, improve your online reputation, and gain more backlinks.

Both On-Page and Off-Page SEO are crucial for a successful SEO strategy. While On-Page SEO helps search engines understand your website and its content, Off-Page SEO helps to establish your website's credibility and authority. Together, they can significantly improve your website's visibility in search engine results.

## D. SEO Tools and Resources

Effective SEO requires the right tools and resources. These can help you conduct keyword research, analyze your website's performance, monitor your rankings, and much more. Here are some of the most popular and effective SEO tools and resources:

Google Keyword Planner: This is a free tool from Google that helps you find keywords related to your business or industry. It shows you how often the keywords are searched and how their search volume changes over time.

SEMrush: This is a comprehensive SEO tool that offers features like keyword research, site audit, backlink analysis, and rank tracking. It also provides insights into your competitors' strategies.

Ahrefs: Similar to SEMrush, Ahrefs is a full-featured SEO tool that provides in-depth analysis of your website, keywords, and backlinks. It's particularly well-known for its backlink analysis feature.

Moz Pro: This is another all-in-one SEO toolset. It offers features like keyword research, SEO audit and crawl, rank tracking, and backlink analysis. Moz Pro also provides a suite of free SEO tools, including MozBar, a browser extension that provides instant SEO insights about any webpage.

Yoast SEO: If you're using WordPress, Yoast SEO is a must-have plugin. It helps you optimize your posts for search engines, provides readability analysis, and even generates an XML sitemap for your site.

Google Analytics: This is a powerful tool that helps you understand your website traffic, user behavior, and a lot more. It's essential for tracking the performance of your SEO efforts.

Google Search Console: This free tool from Google helps you monitor and troubleshoot your website's presence in Google Search results. It shows you which keywords your site is ranking for, identifies crawl errors, and much more.

SEO Guides and Blogs: Resources like the Moz Beginner's Guide to SEO, the Ahrefs Blog, the SEMrush Blog, and the Google Webmaster Central Blog provide a wealth of information on all things SEO.

These tools and resources can provide valuable insights and help you implement effective SEO strategies. However, remember that SEO is not just about tools and tactics. It's about creating high-quality, valuable content that meets the needs of your audience. The tools are just there to help you achieve this goal more effectively.

# VIII. LOCAL SEO AND ALGORITHMS

## A. *Importance of Local SEO*

Local Search Engine Optimization (SEO) is a crucial aspect of digital marketing, particularly for businesses that operate in specific geographic areas. It involves optimizing your online presence to attract more business from relevant local searches on Google and other search engines.

The importance of local SEO cannot be overstated. Here's why:

Visibility: Local SEO helps your business appear in local search results, increasing your visibility to potential customers in your area. When users search for businesses or services near them, you want your business to be one of the first they see.

Relevance: Local SEO helps you reach the customers who are most likely to use your products or services. By targeting users in your area, you're focusing on people who are more likely to convert because your business is convenient for them.

Competitive Edge: Many businesses, especially small and medium-sized ones, have not yet recognized the importance of local SEO. By investing in local SEO, you can gain a competitive edge in your local market.

Mobile Searches: With the increasing use of mobile devices for internet browsing, local SEO has become even more critical. People often use their smartphones to find local businesses while they're on the go, and local SEO ensures you're reaching these mobile users.

Google's Algorithm: Google's algorithm favors local businesses when users make local searches. By optimizing for local SEO, you're aligning your business with Google's ranking factors and improving your chances of ranking high in search results.

In the following sections of the book, we'll delve deeper into the specifics of local SEO and provide strategies for optimizing your business for local searches. We'll also explore how local SEO interacts with the algorithms of major search engines and digital platforms. Understanding how these algorithms work can help you tailor your strategies and maximize your success in local search results.

## B. Strategies for Improving Local SEO

Improving your local SEO involves a combination of on-page, off-page, and technical SEO strategies. Here are some key strategies to consider:

Google My Business: Claim and optimize your Google My Business listing. This is a free tool that allows you to manage how your business appears on Google Search and Maps. Make sure your listing is complete, accurate, and updated regularly.

Online Directories: List your business in online directories and review sites, such as Yelp, TripAdvisor, and Yellow Pages. Ensure your business name, address, and phone number (NAP) are consistent across all listings.

Local Keywords: Incorporate local keywords into your website content and meta tags. These are keywords that include specific geographic locations, such as "coffee shop in Brooklyn" or "plumber in San Francisco."

Reviews: Encourage and respond to customer reviews. Reviews not only influence potential customers but also impact your local search rankings. Google considers the quantity and quality of reviews as a factor in determining local search rankings.

Local Links: Build links with other local businesses, blogs, and community websites. Local link building can help improve your local search visibility and drive more local traffic to your website.

Mobile Optimization: Ensure your website is mobile-friendly. Many local searches are done on mobile devices, and a mobile-friendly website provides a better user experience, which can improve your search rankings.

Schema Markup: Use schema markup (a form of microdata) on your website to provide search engines with more information about your business, such as your address, hours of operation, and the services you offer.

Content Marketing: Create high-quality, locally-focused content. This could include blog posts about local events, a page dedicated to local resources, or guides relevant to your local audience.

# C. Case Studies: Successful Local SEO Campaigns

Examining successful local SEO campaigns can provide valuable insights and inspiration for your own efforts. Here are a few examples:

A Local Bakery's Rise to Fame: A small bakery in Boston was struggling to attract customers beyond their immediate neighborhood. They claimed their Google My Business listing, optimized their website for local keywords, and started actively encouraging customers to leave reviews on Google and Yelp. They also partnered with local food bloggers to create content and build local links. Within six months, they saw a significant increase in their visibility in local search results, leading to increased foot traffic and sales.

A Plumber's Digital Transformation: A plumbing business in San Francisco had relied on word-of-mouth referrals for years. They decided to invest in local SEO to expand their customer base. They updated their website to be mobile-friendly, incorporated local keywords into their content, and listed their business in various online directories. They also used schema markup to provide more information about their services to search engines. As a result, they saw a significant increase in calls from potential customers finding them through local search.

A Boutique Hotel's Online Success: A boutique hotel in Austin wanted to compete with larger hotel chains in the area. They claimed their Google My Business listing and encouraged guests to leave reviews. They also created a blog on their website where they posted about local events and attractions, incorporating local keywords into their posts. They built local links by partnering with local businesses and tourism websites. Their efforts paid off with improved rankings in local search results and increased bookings.

These case studies demonstrate the power of local SEO in driving business success. In the following sections of the book, we'll delve deeper into these strategies and explore how you can apply them to your own business. We'll also explore how these strategies interact with the algorithms of major search engines and digital platforms. Understanding how these algorithms work can help you tailor your strategies and maximize your success in local search results.

# IX. SOCIAL MEDIA ALGORITHMS

# A. Understanding Social Media Algorithms

Social media algorithms are a type of software that sort and present content based on certain parameters or rules. These algorithms play a significant role in determining what content you see and when you see it on your social media feeds.

Each social media platform has its own unique algorithm, and they all share a common goal: to provide users with the most relevant and engaging content. To do this, they analyze a multitude of factors, including:

Personal Behavior: The algorithm takes into account your past behavior on the platform, such as the posts you've liked, shared, or commented on, the accounts you interact with most frequently, and the type of content you engage with.

Post Information: This includes details about the post itself, such as the type of content (photo, video, link, etc.), the posting time, and the engagement it has received (likes, comments, shares, etc.).

Profile Information: The algorithm also considers information about the person or page that posted the content, such as how often you interact with them and the overall engagement their posts receive.

Understanding social media algorithms is crucial for anyone looking to increase their visibility and engagement on social media. Whether you're a business owner looking to reach more customers, a content creator seeking to grow your audience, or a user wanting to understand why you see certain posts in your feed, having a grasp of how these algorithms work can help you make the most of your social media experience.

In the following sections, we'll delve deeper into the algorithms of specific social media platforms, including Facebook, Instagram, Twitter, YouTube, and TikTok, and provide strategies for each platform.

## B. Strategies for Each Platform (Facebook, Instagram, Twitter, YouTube, TikTok)

Each social media platform has its own unique algorithm, which means that strategies that work on one platform may not necessarily work on another. Here are some platform-specific strategies to help you increase your visibility and engagement:

Facebook:

Post Engaging Content: Facebook's algorithm prioritizes posts that spark conversations and meaningful interactions. Ask questions, share useful information, or post content that encourages users to interact.

Use Facebook Live: Facebook's algorithm favors live videos, which often get more engagement than regular videos.

Post at the Right Time: Find out when your audience is most active and post during these times to increase your chances of engagement.
Instagram:

Use Relevant Hashtags: Hashtags can help increase your visibility on Instagram. Use relevant and popular hashtags to reach a wider audience.

Engage with Other Users: Respond to comments on your posts, and engage with other users' content. This can help increase your visibility and followers.

Use Instagram Stories: Instagram's algorithm favors accounts that use all of its features, including Stories. Regularly post engaging content to your Stories to boost your visibility.
Twitter:

Tweet Frequently: Twitter's algorithm favors recent content, so tweet frequently to increase your visibility.

Engage with Other Users: Retweet, reply to tweets, and engage with your followers to increase your reach.

Use Relevant Hashtags: Like Instagram, using relevant hashtags can help increase your visibility on Twitter.

YouTube:

Optimize Your Video Titles and Descriptions: Use relevant keywords in your video titles and descriptions to help YouTube's algorithm understand what your video is about.

Encourage Engagement: Ask viewers to like, comment, and subscribe at the end of your videos. This can help increase your video's visibility.

Create High-Quality Content: YouTube's algorithm favors videos that keep viewers on the platform longer. Create high-quality, engaging content to increase your watch time.
TikTok:

Post Regularly: TikTok's algorithm seems to favor accounts that post regularly. Try to post at least once a day to increase your visibility.

Use Trending Hashtags and Sounds: TikTok's algorithm often promotes videos that use trending hashtags and sounds. Incorporate these into your videos where relevant.

Engage with Other Users: Like other platforms, engaging with other users can help increase your visibility on TikTok.

Remember, these strategies are just a starting point. The best way to understand what works for your specific audience is to experiment with different strategies, monitor your results, and adjust your approach based on what you learn.

# C. Case Studies of Successful Social Media Campaigns

Examining successful social media campaigns can provide valuable insights into how brands effectively leverage social media algorithms to reach their audience. Here are a few examples:

Dove's #SpeakBeautiful Campaign (Twitter): Dove launched the #SpeakBeautiful campaign on Twitter to encourage positive conversations about beauty and body image. The campaign used a custom algorithm to identify negative tweets about beauty and body image, and then Dove responded to these tweets with positive messages. The campaign was a huge success, with a significant decrease in negative tweets about beauty and body image.

Airbnb's #WeAccept Campaign (Facebook): Airbnb used Facebook's algorithm to their advantage by creating a campaign that sparked meaningful conversations. The #WeAccept campaign, which promoted acceptance and inclusivity, was launched with a video that quickly went viral. The campaign received millions of views and thousands of shares, significantly increasing Airbnb's visibility on Facebook.

Gymshark's #Gymshark66 Challenge (Instagram): Gymshark, a fitness apparel brand, launched the #Gymshark66 challenge on Instagram, encouraging followers to make a positive change in their life and post about it on Instagram for 66 days. The campaign leveraged Instagram's algorithm by encouraging user-generated content and engagement, leading to a significant increase in Gymshark's Instagram followers and engagement.

Blendtec's "Will It Blend?" Series (YouTube): Blendtec, a blender manufacturer, created a YouTube series called "Will It Blend?"

where they blended various non-food items, like smartphones and toys, to show the power of their blenders. The videos were entertaining and engaging, leading to millions of views and a significant increase in Blendtec's sales.

Chipotle's #GuacDance Challenge (TikTok): Chipotle leveraged TikTok's algorithm by creating a branded challenge, the #GuacDance challenge, where users were encouraged to do a dance dedicated to Chipotle's guacamole. The campaign was a huge success, with over 250,000 submissions and a significant increase in guacamole sales.

These case studies demonstrate how understanding and leveraging social media algorithms, along with creating engaging and relevant content, can lead to successful social media campaigns.

# X. CONTENT IS KING

## *A. Importance of Quality Content*

The phrase "Content is King" has become a mantra in the digital marketing world, and for good reason. Quality content is the cornerstone of successful digital marketing strategies, from SEO and social media marketing to email marketing and beyond. Here's why quality content is so important:

Engages Your Audience: Quality content engages your audience, keeps them on your website longer, and encourages them to take action, whether that's making a purchase, signing up for a newsletter, or sharing your content with their network.

Improves SEO: Quality content is key to SEO success. Search engines like Google reward websites that provide valuable, relevant content to users. By regularly publishing high-quality content, you can improve your search engine rankings and increase your visibility.

Builds Trust and Authority: By providing valuable content that helps solve problems or answer questions, you can build trust with your audience and position your business as an authority in your field. This can lead to increased customer loyalty and more business over time.

Drives Social Media Success: Quality content is also crucial for social media success. The more valuable and engaging your content is, the more likely it is to be shared, increasing your reach and visibility.

Supports Other Marketing Efforts: Quality content supports all your other marketing efforts. For example, you can repurpose blog posts into email newsletters or social media posts, or use them as resources in your customer service efforts.

In the following sections of the book, we'll delve deeper into the importance of quality content and provide strategies for creating content that resonates with your audience and achieves your marketing goals. We'll also explore how quality content interacts with the algorithms of major search engines and digital platforms. Understanding how these algorithms work can help you tailor your content strategies and maximize your success.

# B. Content Strategies for Different Platforms

Different digital platforms require different content strategies. What works on one platform may not work on another. Here are some strategies for creating content for various platforms:

Website/Blog: Your website or blog is often the first point of contact for potential customers. Focus on creating high-quality, SEO-friendly content that provides value to your audience. This could be informative blog posts, how-to guides, product reviews, or industry news updates.

Facebook: Facebook is a great platform for sharing a mix of content, including blog posts, photos, videos, and company updates. Engage with your audience by asking questions, encouraging comments, and responding to feedback.

Instagram: Instagram is a visually-focused platform, so high-quality images and videos are key. Use Instagram Stories to share behind-the-scenes content, and use hashtags to increase your visibility.

Twitter: Twitter is ideal for sharing short, timely updates and engaging with your audience. Share industry news, company updates, and links to your blog posts. Engage in Twitter chats and use hashtags to join relevant conversations.

LinkedIn: LinkedIn is a professional networking platform, so your content should be industry-focused and professional. Share company news, industry articles, and professional insights. Engage with other businesses and professionals in your industry.

YouTube: YouTube is the second largest search engine after Google, making it a great platform for SEO-friendly video content. Create how-to videos, product demonstrations, customer testimonials, and behind-the-scenes videos.

Pinterest: Pinterest is a platform for sharing and discovering new ideas. Create high-quality images that represent your blog posts, products, or ideas. Use keywords in your descriptions to increase your visibility.

TikTok: TikTok is a platform for short, engaging video content. Create fun and engaging videos that showcase your brand's personality. Participate in trending challenges to increase your visibility.

## C. The Role of Virality in
## Content Creation

The concept of virality plays a significant role in content creation and digital marketing. When a piece of content goes viral, it is shared rapidly and widely across the internet, reaching a large audience in a short period of time. Here's why virality is important and how it can be leveraged in content creation:

Reach: Viral content can reach a large audience, often far beyond your existing followers or customers. This can significantly increase your brand visibility and attract new customers.

Engagement: Viral content often generates high levels of engagement, including likes, comments, shares, and mentions. This can boost your social media metrics and improve your visibility in platform algorithms.

Brand Awareness: When your content goes viral, it can significantly increase awareness of your brand. This can lead to increased recognition and recall of your brand among consumers.

Cost-Effective Marketing: Viral content can be a cost-effective form of marketing. While there's no guarantee that a piece of content will go viral, when it does, it can generate a high return on investment in terms of reach and engagement.

Creating viral content, however, is not an exact science. It often involves a combination of high-quality content, relevance to the audience, timing, and a bit of luck. Some strategies to increase the chances of your content going viral include creating emotionally engaging content, leveraging trending topics, incorporating compelling visuals, and encouraging users to share your content.

# XI. VIDEO CONTENT
# AND ALGORITHMS

# A. The Rise of Video Content

In recent years, video content has seen a meteoric rise in popularity and effectiveness, becoming a dominant force in the digital landscape. This rise can be attributed to several factors:

Increased Engagement: Video content is highly engaging. It has the ability to convey a large amount of information quickly and effectively, making it easier for audiences to absorb and retain the information.

Technological Advancements: The proliferation of high-speed internet and advanced mobile devices has made it easier than ever for people to consume video content, anytime and anywhere.

Social Media Platforms: Social media platforms have heavily prioritized video content. Features like Facebook's auto-play videos, Instagram's IGTV, YouTube's recommendation algorithm, and the rise of TikTok, have all contributed to the popularity of video content.

SEO Benefits: Search engines love video content. Websites with video content are more likely to rank higher in search results, making video a powerful tool for SEO.

Higher Conversion Rates: Video content has been shown to drive higher conversion rates. According to a study by HubSpot, including a video on a landing page can increase conversions by up to 80%.

Versatility: Video content is incredibly versatile. It can be used for a variety of purposes, from product demonstrations and how-to guides, to customer testimonials and brand stories.

The rise of video content has significant implications for algorithms. As platforms prioritize video content, understanding how to create and optimize your videos for these algorithms is becoming increasingly important. In the following sections, we'll delve deeper into the world of video algorithms and provide strategies for optimizing your video content.

## B. Understanding Video Algorithms
## on Various Platforms

Just as with text-based content, video content is also subject to the algorithms of various platforms. Each platform has its own unique algorithm that determines how videos are discovered and recommended to users. Here's a brief overview of how video algorithms work on some of the major platforms:

YouTube: YouTube's algorithm recommends videos based on a user's viewing history, liked videos, and engagement (comments and shares). It also considers the relevance of a video's title, description, and tags to the user's search queries or interests. The algorithm also prioritizes videos that lead to longer overall watch time on YouTube.

Facebook: Facebook's algorithm prioritizes videos that receive a lot of engagement, especially within a short time of being posted. It also favors longer videos that keep people watching. Facebook Live videos are also given priority in the news feed.

Instagram: Instagram's algorithm considers factors like the likelihood the user will be interested in the content, the timeliness of the post, and the user's interactions with the person posting. Videos that receive more likes, comments, shares, and views are more likely to appear higher up in the user's feed or on the Explore page.

TikTok: TikTok's algorithm is unique in that it prioritizes content discovery, making it possible for videos from unknown users to go viral. The algorithm considers factors like user interactions (such as shares, likes, and comments), video details (like hashtags, details, and whether the content is in line with TikTok's guidelines), and device and account settings (like location, language preference, and device type).

LinkedIn: LinkedIn's algorithm prioritizes content that is likely to generate engagement, considering factors like the connections between the poster and viewer, the relevance of the content to the viewer, and the likelihood that the viewer will share or comment on the post.

Understanding these algorithms is crucial for anyone looking to increase their visibility and engagement on these platforms. In the next section, we'll provide strategies for optimizing your video content for these algorithms.

# C. Strategies for Optimizing Video Content

Optimizing your video content for various platform algorithms can significantly increase your visibility and engagement. Here are some strategies to help you do just that:

Create High-Quality Content: This is the most important factor. No matter how well you optimize your video, if the content is not high-quality and engaging, it won't perform well. Make sure your video is clear, concise, and provides value to your audience.

Use Relevant Keywords: Just like with text-based content, using relevant keywords in your video title, description, and tags can help algorithms understand what your video is about and show it to users who are interested in those topics.

Encourage Engagement: Encourage viewers to like, comment, share, and subscribe. This not only increases your engagement but also signals to the algorithm that your content is valuable.

Optimize for Mobile: With more and more people consuming video content on their mobile devices, it's important to ensure that your videos are optimized for mobile viewing.

Use Thumbnails and Captions: A compelling thumbnail can significantly increase your video's click-through rate. Also, adding captions to your videos can improve accessibility and boost your SEO.

Post Regularly: Algorithms favor accounts that post regularly. Try to maintain a consistent posting schedule to keep your audience engaged and coming back for more.

Analyze Your Performance: Use analytics tools to understand which of your videos are performing well and why. This can provide valuable insights that you can use to optimize your future videos.

Remember, each platform has its own unique algorithm, so what works on one platform may not necessarily work on another. It's important to understand the specific algorithm of each platform and tailor your strategy accordingly.

# XII. DATA ANALYSIS AND INSIGHTS

## A. Importance of Data in Digital Marketing

Data is the lifeblood of digital marketing. It provides insights into your audience, your performance, and the effectiveness of your strategies. Here's why data is so important in digital marketing:

Understanding Your Audience: Data can provide valuable insights into your audience, including their demographics, interests, behaviors, and preferences. This can help you tailor your marketing strategies to better meet their needs and interests.

Measuring Performance: Data allows you to measure the performance of your marketing strategies. You can track metrics like website traffic, social media engagement, email open rates, conversion rates, and more. This can help you understand what's working and what's not, so you can adjust your strategies accordingly.

Identifying Trends: Data can help you identify trends in your industry or market. This can help you stay ahead of the curve and take advantage of new opportunities.

Personalization: Data can enable you to personalize your marketing efforts. By understanding your audience's preferences and behaviors, you can deliver personalized content, recommendations, and offers that are more likely to engage and convert them.

Decision Making: Data can inform your decision-making process. By analyzing data, you can make evidence-based decisions that are more likely to lead to successful outcomes.

In the following sections of the book, we'll delve deeper into the importance of data in digital marketing and provide strategies for collecting, analyzing, and leveraging data. We'll also explore how data interacts with the algorithms of major digital platforms. Understanding how these algorithms work can help you tailor your data strategies and maximize your success.

## B. Tools for Tracking and Analyzing Performance

Tracking and analyzing your performance is crucial for understanding the effectiveness of your digital marketing strategies. Fortunately, there are many tools available that can help you collect and analyze data. Here are some key tools to consider:

Google Analytics: This is a powerful tool for tracking and analyzing website traffic. It provides insights into how users find and interact with your website, allowing you to understand user behavior and optimize your website for better performance.

Google Search Console: This tool provides insights into your website's visibility in Google's search results. It can help you understand how Google's search engine sees your site, identify issues that might be affecting your visibility, and optimize your site for better search performance.

Social Media Analytics: Most social media platforms provide built-in analytics tools that provide insights into your social media performance. These tools can help you understand your audience, track engagement, and optimize your social media strategies.

Email Marketing Analytics: Email marketing platforms typically provide analytics features that allow you to track open rates, click-through rates, conversions, and other key email marketing metrics.

SEO Tools: Tools like SEMrush, Ahrefs, and Moz provide a wealth of data for SEO analysis, including keyword rankings, backlink analysis, and competitive analysis.

Customer Relationship Management (CRM) Systems: CRM systems like Salesforce and HubSpot can provide valuable insights into your customer interactions, helping you understand your customer journey and optimize your marketing strategies for better customer engagement and retention.

Heatmap Tools: Tools like Hotjar and Crazy Egg provide heatmaps, scroll maps, and other visualizations that show how users interact with your website. This can help you understand user behavior and optimize your site design for better user experience and conversion rates.

## C. Interpreting Data and Making Informed Decisions

Interpreting data correctly and making informed decisions based on that data is a critical skill in digital marketing. Here are some key considerations:

Understand Your Metrics: Before you can interpret data, you need to understand what the metrics mean. For example, in Google Analytics, metrics like bounce rate, session duration, and pages per session can tell you a lot about user behavior on your website.

Context is Key: Always interpret data in context. For instance, a high bounce rate might initially seem like a bad thing, but if the goal of the page is to quickly provide information or direct users to a different site, a high bounce rate might actually indicate success.

Look for Trends: Instead of focusing on individual data points, look for trends over time. This can provide more meaningful insights into your performance and help you identify issues or opportunities.

Segment Your Data: Segmenting your data can provide more granular insights. For example, you might segment your website traffic by source to understand which channels are driving the most traffic, or segment your social media engagement by post type to see what kind of content resonates most with your audience.

Test and Learn: Use your data to inform experiments, then measure the results. For example, if your data shows that your email open rates are low, you might test different subject lines to see what improves open rates.

Make Data-Driven Decisions: Use your data to inform your decision-making process. If your data shows that one marketing channel is outperforming others, you might decide to allocate more of your budget to that channel.

# XIII.
# PERSONALIZATION
# AND ALGORITHMS

# A. The Role of Personalization in Algorithms

Personalization plays a significant role in the functioning of algorithms, especially in the context of digital marketing and content delivery. The goal of personalization is to tailor the user's experience to their specific interests, behaviors, and needs. This is achieved by using data to understand the user's preferences and delivering content that aligns with those preferences.

Algorithms play a crucial role in this personalization process. They analyze vast amounts of data, including a user's browsing history, search queries, interaction with previous content, location, and even the time of day to deliver a personalized user experience.

For instance, when you search for something on Google, the algorithm doesn't just consider the relevance of web pages to your search query. It also considers your past search history, your location, and many other factors to deliver personalized search results.

Similarly, on social media platforms like Facebook or Instagram, the algorithm analyzes your interactions with previous posts (such as likes, comments, and shares) to show you more content that you're likely to be interested in.

E-commerce platforms like Amazon use algorithms to recommend products based on your past purchases and browsing behavior. Even streaming platforms like Netflix and Spotify use algorithms to recommend movies, TV shows, or music based on what you've watched or listened to in the past.

In all these cases, the goal of the algorithm is to improve the user experience by delivering personalized content that the user will find relevant and engaging. In the next sections, we'll discuss how to leverage personalization for better visibility and provide some successful case studies.

## B. How to Leverage Personalization
## for Better Visibility

Leveraging personalization can significantly improve your visibility online by delivering more relevant and engaging content to your audience. Here are some strategies to help you leverage personalization:

Understand Your Audience: The first step in personalization is understanding your audience. Use analytics tools to gather data on your audience's behavior, interests, and preferences. This can help you tailor your content to their specific needs and interests.

Segment Your Audience: Not all your users are the same. Segment your audience based on factors like demographics, behavior, and interests. This allows you to deliver more targeted and personalized content to each segment.

Personalize Your Content: Use the data you've gathered to personalize your content. This could be as simple as using the user's name in your communication, or as complex as recommending products or content based on their past behavior.

Use Personalized CTAs: Personalized calls-to-action (CTAs) can significantly improve your conversion rates. For example, instead of a generic "Buy Now" button, a personalized CTA might say "Buy Now and Get 10% Off Your First Order".

Leverage AI and Machine Learning: AI and machine learning technologies can analyze vast amounts of data and deliver personalized experiences at scale. Many platforms now offer AI-powered personalization features that you can leverage.

Test and Optimize: Personalization is not a set-it-and-forget-it strategy. It's important to continually test your personalization efforts, analyze the results, and optimize based on your findings.

Remember, the goal of personalization is to improve the user experience. Always respect your users' privacy and be transparent about how you're using their data. Personalization should be about delivering value to the user, not just pushing your own agenda.

# C. Case Studies: Successful Personalization Strategies

Examining successful personalization strategies can provide valuable insights into how brands effectively leverage personalization to improve visibility and engagement. Here are a few examples:

Netflix's Personalized Recommendations: Netflix uses a sophisticated algorithm to recommend movies and TV shows based on a user's viewing history. This personalized approach has not only improved user engagement but also increased viewer retention.

Spotify's Discover Weekly: Spotify's Discover Weekly playlist is a personalized playlist that's updated every week with songs that the algorithm predicts the user will enjoy. This feature has been a huge hit, with millions of users tuning in every week.

Amazon's Product Recommendations: Amazon uses personalization to recommend products based on a user's browsing history, past purchases, and items in their shopping cart. This strategy has significantly increased Amazon's sales and improved the user experience.

Starbucks' Mobile App: Starbucks uses its mobile app to deliver personalized offers to its customers. The app uses data like purchase history and location to tailor offers to each user's specific preferences.

Cadbury's Personalized Video Campaign: Cadbury created a personalized video campaign on Facebook where users could create and share a personalized video with their friends featuring a Cadbury Dairy Milk bar with their friend's name on it. The campaign was a huge success, with a significant increase in engagement and sales.

These case studies demonstrate how personalization, when done right, can significantly improve visibility and engagement. By understanding your audience and delivering personalized experiences that meet their specific needs and interests, you can create a more engaging and effective online presence.

# XIV. PAID ADVERTISING AND ALGORITHMS

# A. Overview of Paid
# Online Advertising

Paid online advertising is a key component of many digital marketing strategies. It involves paying to display your advertisements or promotional content on digital platforms, including search engines, social media platforms, and other websites. Here's an overview of the main types of paid online advertising:

Pay-Per-Click (PPC) Advertising: This is a model of online advertising where you pay a fee each time one of your ads is clicked. Google Ads is one of the most popular platforms for PPC advertising, allowing you to display ads in Google's search results and on other Google properties.

Social Media Advertising: Most social media platforms offer advertising options that allow you to reach their users. For example, Facebook Ads allows you to target users based on a wide range of criteria, including demographics, interests, and behaviors.

Display Advertising: This involves displaying visual ads on websites or digital platforms. These ads can come in many formats, including banners, video ads, and native ads.

Retargeting/Remarketing: This is a strategy that involves showing ads to people who have previously interacted with your website or digital content. This can be a highly effective way to re-engage potential customers who have shown an interest in your products or services.

Influencer Marketing: This involves partnering with influencers (people with a large and engaged following on social media) to promote your products or services. While not traditionally considered advertising, it is a paid strategy that can be highly effective for reaching certain audiences.

Affiliate Marketing: This involves paying affiliates (third-party individuals or companies) a commission for promoting your products or services and driving sales.

In the following sections of the book, we'll delve deeper into these types of paid online advertising and provide strategies for using them effectively. We'll also explore how these advertising methods interact with the algorithms of major digital platforms. Understanding how these algorithms work can help you tailor your advertising strategies and maximize your return on investment.

## B. How Algorithms Affect
## Ad Performance

Algorithms play a crucial role in determining the performance of your online ads. They decide who sees your ads, when they see them, and how often they see them. Here's how algorithms can affect your ad performance:

Ad Ranking: Most online advertising platforms use an auction system to decide which ads to display. The algorithm ranks ads based on a variety of factors, including the amount you're willing to pay per click (bid), the relevance of your ad to the user (quality score), and the expected impact of your ad.

Targeting: Algorithms use the targeting criteria you set (like demographics, interests, behaviors, and location) to decide who sees your ads. The more accurately you can define your target audience, the more effectively the algorithm can match your ads to potential customers.

Personalization: Algorithms use data about users (like their browsing history, search queries, and social media activity) to personalize the ads they see. This can make your ads more relevant and increase their performance.

Optimization: Over time, algorithms learn which ads perform best and optimize your campaigns accordingly. They may adjust your ad delivery to maximize results based on your campaign objective (like clicks, conversions, or impressions).

A/B Testing: Algorithms can also help you test different versions of your ads to see which perform best. They can automatically adjust your ad delivery based on the results of these tests.

Understanding how these algorithms work can help you create more effective ads and get a better return on your advertising spend. In the following sections of the book, we'll delve deeper into these concepts and provide strategies for working with algorithms to optimize your ad performance.

# C. Strategies for Optimizing Ad Spend

Optimizing your ad spend involves getting the most value from your advertising budget. Here are some strategies to help you optimize your ad spend:

Set Clear Objectives: Before you start advertising, define what you want to achieve. Your objectives could be increasing brand awareness, driving traffic to your website, generating leads, or driving sales. Having clear objectives can help you measure the success of your campaigns and optimize your ad spend.

Target Precisely: Use the targeting options provided by the advertising platform to reach your ideal audience. The more precisely you can target your ads, the more effective they're likely to be, and the better your return on investment.

Use A/B Testing: Test different versions of your ads to see which perform best. You can test different headlines, ad copy, images, calls to action, and more. Use the results of your tests to optimize your ads and your ad spend.

Monitor and Adjust: Regularly monitor the performance of your ads and adjust your strategies as needed. If an ad isn't performing well, try adjusting its targeting, content, or bidding strategy.

Leverage Automation: Many advertising platforms offer automation features that can help you optimize your ad spend. For example, Google Ads has an automated bidding feature that adjusts your bids in real time to maximize your results.

Optimize for Conversions: Focus on driving actions that have a direct impact on your bottom line. This could be product purchases, lead form submissions, or app downloads, depending on your business. Use conversion tracking to measure these actions and optimize your ads to drive more of them.

# XV. E-COMMERCE AND ALGORITHMS

## A. Role of Algorithms in E-commerce

Algorithms play a crucial role in the functioning of e-commerce platforms. They are used to analyze vast amounts of data to deliver personalized shopping experiences, recommend products, predict trends, optimize pricing, manage inventory, and much more.

Here are some ways in which algorithms are used in e-commerce:

Product Recommendations: Algorithms analyze a customer's browsing history, past purchases, and other behaviors to recommend products they might be interested in. This not only improves the shopping experience for the customer but also increases sales for the e-commerce platform.

Search Results: When a customer searches for a product, the algorithm determines which products to display in the search results based on relevance, customer reviews, sales history, and other factors.

Pricing Optimization: Algorithms can analyze market trends, demand, competition, and other factors to optimize pricing and maximize profits.

Inventory Management: Algorithms can predict demand for different products and help manage inventory accordingly, reducing storage costs and preventing stockouts or overstocking.

Fraud Detection: Algorithms can analyze patterns in order data to detect fraudulent transactions and protect both the e-commerce platform and its customers.

Customer Segmentation: Algorithms can segment customers based on their behavior, preferences, and other factors, enabling more targeted marketing and improved customer service.

In the era of online shopping, algorithms have become an

indispensable tool for e-commerce platforms. They enable a level of personalization, efficiency, and security that would be impossible to achieve otherwise. In the following sections, we'll discuss how to optimize e-commerce platforms for better visibility and provide some successful case studies.

## B. Optimizing E-commerce Platforms for Better Visibility

Optimizing your e-commerce platform can significantly improve your visibility online, leading to increased traffic, higher conversion rates, and ultimately, more sales. Here are some strategies to help you optimize your e-commerce platform:

SEO: Just like any other website, your e-commerce platform needs to be optimized for search engines. This includes using relevant keywords in your product titles and descriptions, optimizing your site structure, and creating high-quality, valuable content.

Mobile Optimization: With more and more people shopping on their mobile devices, it's crucial to ensure that your e-commerce platform is optimized for mobile. This includes having a responsive design, ensuring your site loads quickly, and making it easy for users to navigate and make purchases on their mobile devices.

User Experience: A good user experience is crucial for keeping visitors on your site and encouraging them to make a purchase. This includes having a clean, easy-to-navigate design, providing clear and detailed product information, and making the checkout process as simple as possible.

Personalization: Use algorithms to deliver a personalized shopping experience. This could include recommending products based on a user's browsing history or personalizing your communication with each user.

Social Proof: Social proof, such as customer reviews and testimonials, can significantly improve your conversion rates. Encourage your customers to leave reviews, and display these reviews prominently on your site.

Analytics: Use analytics tools to understand how users are interacting with your site, which products are selling well, and where there's room for improvement. Use this data to optimize your e-commerce platform and improve your results.

Remember, the goal of optimization is not just to increase your visibility, but also to improve the shopping experience for your customers. By focusing on both these aspects, you can create a successful e-commerce platform that attracts and retains customers.

## C. Case Studies: Successful E-commerce SEO Strategies

Examining successful e-commerce SEO strategies can provide valuable insights into how brands effectively leverage SEO to improve visibility and increase sales. Here are a few examples:

Zappos: Zappos, an online shoe and clothing retailer, has a comprehensive SEO strategy that includes a well-structured site, detailed product descriptions with relevant keywords, and a strong focus on customer reviews for social proof. This has helped Zappos consistently rank high in search results for a wide range of keywords.

Etsy: Etsy, a global marketplace for unique and creative goods, has a strong SEO strategy that includes a focus on long-tail keywords. Sellers are encouraged to use specific, descriptive titles and tags for their products, which helps Etsy rank for a wide range of niche search terms.

Wayfair: Wayfair, an online home goods store, uses a combination of detailed product descriptions, user-generated reviews, and high-quality images to optimize their product pages for search engines. They also have a comprehensive content marketing strategy that includes buying guides, how-to articles, and other valuable content that attracts organic traffic.

ASOS: ASOS, a British online fashion and cosmetic retailer, uses a variety of SEO strategies, including a mobile-optimized site, detailed product descriptions with relevant keywords, and a strong internal linking structure. They also leverage user-generated content, such as customer reviews and photos, to boost their SEO.

Amazon: Amazon's SEO strategy is multifaceted, including a focus on long-tail keywords in product titles and descriptions, user-generated reviews, and a highly efficient site structure. Amazon also leverages its vast amount of user data to provide personalized product recommendations, further enhancing its SEO.

These case studies demonstrate that a successful e-commerce SEO strategy involves a combination of well-structured site, keyword optimization, user-generated content, and a focus on providing a great user experience. By implementing these strategies, e-commerce businesses can improve their visibility in search results, attract more organic traffic, and increase sales.

# XVI. ALGORITHM UPDATES AND PENALTIES

## A. Understanding Algorithm Updates

Algorithm updates are changes made by digital platforms to their algorithms, which can impact how content is ranked and displayed. These updates are made to improve the user experience, combat spam, and keep the platform relevant and useful. Here's what you need to know about algorithm updates:

Frequency: Algorithm updates can happen frequently. Some platforms, like Google, make hundreds of minor updates each year, along with a few major updates. These updates can affect search rankings and visibility.

Impact: The impact of an algorithm update can vary. Some updates might have a minor impact on your visibility, while others can cause significant changes in your rankings. The impact often depends on what the update is targeting and how your content aligns with those changes.

Communication: Some platforms announce major algorithm updates, providing some information about what the update targets. However, many updates are not announced, and the specifics of what an algorithm targets are often not disclosed.

Adaptation: When an algorithm update happens, it's important to monitor your metrics closely to understand its impact on your performance. You may need to adapt your strategies to align with the changes.

Understanding algorithm updates can help you stay ahead in the ever-changing digital landscape. In the following sections of the book, we'll delve deeper into the topic of algorithm updates, provide strategies for adapting to these changes, and discuss how to recover from potential penalties associated with updates.

## B. How to Recover from
## Algorithmic Penalties

Algorithmic penalties are actions taken by digital platforms that negatively impact your visibility or rankings due to violations of their guidelines. Recovering from these penalties requires understanding why you were penalized and taking corrective action. Here's a general process for recovery:

Identify the Penalty: The first step in recovery is identifying that you've been hit by a penalty. This usually involves a sudden drop in your rankings or traffic. Some platforms, like Google, will notify you of a penalty through their webmaster tools.

Understand the Reason: Once you've identified the penalty, you need to understand why it was applied. This could be due to a variety of reasons, such as spammy content, unnatural links, or poor user experience. The notification from the platform may provide some insight into the reason for the penalty.

Take Corrective Action: After understanding the reason for the penalty, you need to take corrective action. This could involve removing or improving spammy content, disavowing unnatural links, improving your website's user experience, or other actions depending on the reason for the penalty.

Submit a Reconsideration Request: After you've taken corrective action, you can submit a reconsideration request to the platform. This is a request for the platform to review your website and potentially lift the penalty. It's important to detail the actions you've taken to correct the issues in your reconsideration request.

Monitor Your Performance: After submitting a reconsideration request, monitor your performance closely. If the penalty is lifted, you should see a recovery in your rankings and traffic. If not, you may need to take further action.

Recovering from an algorithmic penalty can be a complex and time-consuming process, but it's crucial for restoring your visibility and rankings. In the following sections of the book, we'll delve deeper into the topic of algorithmic penalties, provide more detailed recovery strategies, and discuss how to avoid penalties in the first place.

## C. Staying Ahead: Preparing for Future Updates

Staying ahead of algorithm updates and avoiding penalties requires a proactive approach. Here are some strategies to help you prepare for future updates:

Follow Best Practices: Adhere to the best practices recommended by each platform. This includes creating high-quality, relevant content, providing a good user experience, and avoiding tactics that attempt to manipulate rankings.

Stay Informed: Follow industry news and updates from the platforms themselves to stay informed about potential algorithm updates. This can help you anticipate changes and adapt your strategies accordingly.

Monitor Your Performance: Regularly monitor your performance metrics to identify any sudden changes that could indicate an algorithm update or penalty. This can help you respond quickly and minimize the impact on your visibility and rankings.

Diversify Your Strategies: Don't rely too heavily on a single platform or strategy. By diversifying your digital marketing strategies, you can mitigate the impact of an algorithm update on any one platform.

Focus on the User: Ultimately, most algorithm updates aim to improve the user experience. By focusing on providing value to your users — with relevant, high-quality content and a good user experience — you can align your strategies with the goals of the algorithms.

# XVII. FUTURE OF ALGORITHMS

## *A. Predicted Trends in Algorithms*

As technology continues to evolve, so too will the algorithms that power our digital world. Here are some predicted trends in algorithms for the future:

Increased Personalization: As data collection methods become more sophisticated, algorithms will be able to deliver even more personalized experiences. This could include more accurate product recommendations, personalized content feeds, and even personalized search results.

Greater Use of AI and Machine Learning: AI and machine learning technologies are becoming increasingly advanced and will play an even larger role in algorithms. This could lead to more efficient data processing, more accurate predictions, and more intelligent automation.

Ethical and Fair Algorithms: As awareness of the biases and discrimination that can be perpetuated by algorithms grows, there will be an increased focus on creating ethical and fair algorithms. This could include measures to ensure transparency, accountability, and fairness in algorithmic decision-making.

Privacy-Preserving Algorithms: With growing concerns about data privacy, we can expect to see the development of more privacy-preserving algorithms. These algorithms can analyze and make predictions from data without compromising the privacy of individuals.

Real-Time Algorithms: As the demand for real-time information and services grows, so too will the need for real-time algorithms. These algorithms can process and analyze data in real-time, providing up-to-the-minute insights and responses.

Quantum Algorithms: With the advent of quantum computing, we may see the development of quantum algorithms that can solve complex problems much more quickly than traditional algorithms.

These trends point towards a future where algorithms are more personalized, intelligent, ethical, and efficient. However, they also highlight the need for ongoing discussions about the ethical implications of these technologies, including issues of privacy, fairness, and transparency.

# B. Preparing for Changes in Algorithms

As algorithms continue to evolve, it's important for businesses and individuals to stay ahead of these changes. Here are some strategies for preparing for changes in algorithms:

Stay Informed: Keep up-to-date with the latest news and trends in technology and digital marketing. This can help you anticipate changes in algorithms and adjust your strategies accordingly.

Adapt Quickly: When changes to algorithms are announced, be ready to adapt your strategies quickly. This could involve testing new features, adjusting your content, or changing your SEO strategies.

Diversify Your Strategies: Don't rely too heavily on one platform or strategy. By diversifying your digital marketing strategies, you can mitigate the impact of changes to any one algorithm.

Focus on Quality: While the specifics of algorithms may change, the focus on quality content remains constant. Continue to create high-quality, valuable content that meets the needs of your audience.

Use Data: Use data to understand the impact of algorithm changes on your performance. This can help you identify what's working, what's not, and where you need to adjust your strategies.

Consider the Ethical Implications: As you adapt to changes in algorithms, consider the ethical implications of your strategies. This includes respecting user privacy, promoting fairness, and being transparent about your use of data.

By staying informed, adapting quickly, and focusing on quality, you can navigate changes in algorithms and continue to succeed in the digital landscape.

## C. Staying Updated and Adapted to Changes

Staying updated and adapting to changes in algorithms is crucial for maintaining and improving your visibility and engagement online. Here are some strategies to help you stay updated and adapt effectively:

Follow Industry News: Subscribe to industry newsletters, follow relevant blogs, and join professional groups or forums. These resources can provide you with the latest news and insights on changes in algorithms.

Attend Webinars and Conferences: Many platforms and industry organizations host webinars and conferences that can provide valuable insights into upcoming changes and best practices for adapting to these changes.

Leverage Analytics: Use analytics tools to monitor your performance and identify any changes that could be due to updates in algorithms. This can help you understand the impact of algorithm changes on your performance and identify areas where you need to adjust your strategies.

Test and Experiment: Don't be afraid to test and experiment with different strategies. What worked in the past may not work in the future, and experimenting can help you discover new strategies that are more effective.

Seek Expert Advice: If you're unsure how to adapt to changes in algorithms, consider seeking advice from experts. This could be a digital marketing consultant, an SEO expert, or a data scientist.

Focus on Your Audience: Regardless of changes in algorithms, your primary focus should always be your audience. Continue to create high-quality, valuable content that meets the needs of your audience, and you'll be well-positioned to succeed, no matter how algorithms change.

Remember, adapting to changes in algorithms is not a one-time effort, but an ongoing process. By staying informed, monitoring your performance, and continuously adjusting your strategies, you can stay ahead of the curve and continue to succeed in the ever-changing digital landscape.

# XVIII. CONCLUSION

## A. Recap of Key Strategies

As we conclude this comprehensive guide on navigating the world of algorithms in digital marketing, let's recap some of the key strategies we've discussed:

Understanding Algorithms: Grasping how different platform-specific algorithms work is the first step towards leveraging them for your benefit. This includes algorithms of search engines like Google, and social media platforms like Facebook, Instagram, Twitter, YouTube, and TikTok.

Ethics of Algorithms: Being aware of the ethical considerations in algorithm design, such as bias and discrimination, and advocating for fair algorithms is crucial.

SEO and Local SEO: Implementing both general and local SEO strategies can significantly improve your visibility on search engines.

Content Creation: Creating high-quality, relevant content is key. Understanding the role of virality in content creation can help your content reach a wider audience.

Data Analysis and Insights: Collecting, analyzing, and leveraging data can provide valuable insights into your audience, your performance, and the effectiveness of your strategies.

Personalization and Algorithms: Personalizing your marketing efforts based on user behavior and preferences can lead to better visibility and engagement.

Paid Advertising and Algorithms: Understanding how algorithms affect ad performance can help you optimize your ad spend and get a better return on your advertising investment.

Algorithm Updates and Penalties: Staying informed about algorithm updates, understanding how to recover from algorithmic penalties, and preparing for future updates can help you maintain your visibility and rankings.

# B. Encouragement for the Journey Ahead

As we wrap up this guide, I want to take a moment to acknowledge the journey you're embarking on. Navigating the world of algorithms and digital marketing is no small feat. It requires constant learning, adaptation, and resilience. But remember, every step you take is a step towards mastering this dynamic landscape.

The world of algorithms is complex, but it's also full of opportunities. With the right knowledge and strategies, you can leverage algorithms to reach a wider audience, engage more effectively with your customers, and drive your business's growth.

Remember, success doesn't come overnight. It's the result of consistent effort, testing, learning from mistakes, and making incremental improvements. Don't be discouraged by initial challenges or setbacks. They're part of the journey and provide valuable learning opportunities.

Stay curious, stay informed, and stay focused on your goals. The digital landscape is constantly evolving, and so should your strategies. Keep learning, keep experimenting, and keep pushing forward. You've got this!

## C. Final Thoughts and Next Steps

As we close this comprehensive guide, it's time to look ahead and consider your next steps. Here are some final thoughts and suggestions:

Apply What You've Learned: Knowledge is power, but it's the application of knowledge that brings about change. Start applying the strategies and insights you've learned from this book to your digital marketing efforts.

Keep Learning: The digital landscape and its algorithms are constantly evolving. Stay informed about the latest trends, updates, and best practices. Attend webinars, read industry blogs, join online communities, and continue to educate yourself.

Experiment and Adapt: Don't be afraid to try new strategies and techniques. Experimentation is key in digital marketing. Monitor your results, learn from your successes and failures, and continually adapt your strategies.

Measure Your Success: Set clear, measurable goals for your digital marketing efforts. Use the tools and techniques discussed in this book to track your progress and measure your success.

Seek Professional Help if Needed: If you're feeling overwhelmed or unsure about implementing these strategies, consider seeking help from a digital marketing professional or agency. They can provide expert guidance and help you navigate the complexities of algorithms.

Remember, mastering algorithms is a journey, not a destination. It's a continuous process of learning, applying, analyzing, and adapting. But with persistence and the right strategies, you can leverage algorithms to your advantage and achieve your digital marketing goals.

As your journey continues, we hope this book will serve as a valuable resource that you can return to again and again. We wish you every success in your digital marketing endeavors!

# XIX. APPENDICES

# A. *Glossary of Key Terms*

Algorithm: A set of rules or procedures for solving a problem or accomplishing a task, often used by search engines and social media platforms to rank and display content.

Artificial Intelligence (AI): The simulation of human intelligence processes by machines, especially computer systems. These processes include learning, reasoning, problem-solving, perception, and language understanding.

E-commerce: The buying and selling of goods or services using the internet, and the transfer of money and data to execute these transactions.

Engagement: The interaction between users and content online, often measured by actions like likes, shares, comments, and clicks.

Keyword: A word or phrase that describes the content on a page. Keywords are used by search engines to index a page, and by users to find relevant pages.

Machine Learning: A type of artificial intelligence that enables computers to learn and make decisions without being explicitly programmed.

Personalization: The process of tailoring services or products to individual user's characteristics or preferences.

Search Engine Optimization (SEO): The practice of increasing the quantity and quality of traffic to your website through organic search engine results.

Social Proof: The concept that people will follow the actions of the majority, based on the assumption that these actions reflect the correct behavior.

User Behavior: The way users interact with a website or app, including what they click on, how long they spend on each page, and what actions they take.

# B. Recommended Resources and Tools

Here are some recommended resources and tools that can help you understand and leverage algorithms for better online visibility:

Google Analytics: A powerful tool for understanding your website traffic, user behavior, and the effectiveness of your SEO efforts.

SEMrush: A comprehensive tool for keyword research, competitor analysis, SEO audit, and more.

Moz: Offers a suite of tools for keyword research, SEO audit, and link building. Their blog is also a great resource for staying updated on the latest SEO trends and best practices.

Ahrefs: A toolset for backlinks and SEO analysis. It's a great resource for understanding your website's backlink profile and identifying opportunities for improvement.

BuzzSumo: A tool for content research and monitoring. It can help you identify trending topics, find popular content, and track your content's performance.

Hootsuite or Buffer: Social media management tools that allow you to schedule posts, monitor social media conversations, and analyze your social media performance.

Google Trends: A free tool from Google that allows you to see how search query volume changes over time. It's a great resource for identifying trending topics and understanding seasonal fluctuations in search volume.

HubSpot: A comprehensive platform for inbound marketing, sales, and customer service. It offers tools for content management, social media marketing, web analytics, and more.

MailChimp: An email marketing platform that allows you to create, send, and analyze email campaigns.

Yoast SEO: A WordPress plugin that helps you optimize your website for search engines.

These tools can provide valuable insights into your online visibility, help you optimize your content for algorithms, and track your performance over time. However, remember that tools are just that - tools. They are there to help you, but the success of your digital marketing efforts ultimately depends on your strategy and execution.

# C. Further Reading

To continue your learning journey and delve deeper into the world of algorithms and digital marketing, here are some recommended books and resources:

"The Art of SEO" by Eric Enge, Stephan Spencer, and Jessie Stricchiola: This comprehensive guide offers an in-depth look at search engine optimization, including strategies for navigating Google's algorithm.

"Everybody Lies: Big Data, New Data, and What the Internet Can Tell Us About Who We Really Are" by Seth Stephens-Davidowitz: This book explores how data from the internet can reveal fascinating insights about human behavior.

"Weapons of Math Destruction: How Big Data Increases Inequality and Threatens Democracy" by Cathy O'Neil: This book explores the dark side of algorithms and their impact on society.

"Marketing in the Age of Google" by Vanessa Fox: This book provides strategies for leveraging Google's algorithm to improve your visibility and reach your audience.

"The Filter Bubble: How the New Personalized Web Is Changing What We Read and How We Think" by Eli Pariser: This book explores how personalization algorithms shape our online experience and influence our perceptions of the world.

"Hooked: How to Build Habit-Forming Products" by Nir Eyal: This book provides insights into how products can leverage user habits to drive engagement.

"Influence: The Psychology of Persuasion" by Robert Cialdini: While not specifically about algorithms, this book provides valuable insights into the principles of persuasion, which can inform your digital marketing strategies.

"Data-Driven Marketing: The 15 Metrics Everyone in Marketing Should Know" by Mark Jeffery: This book provides a comprehensive overview of key marketing metrics and how to use them to drive success.

Remember, the key to mastering algorithms and digital marketing is continuous learning. These resources can provide further insights and strategies to help you navigate the ever-changing digital landscape.

☆☆☆☆☆